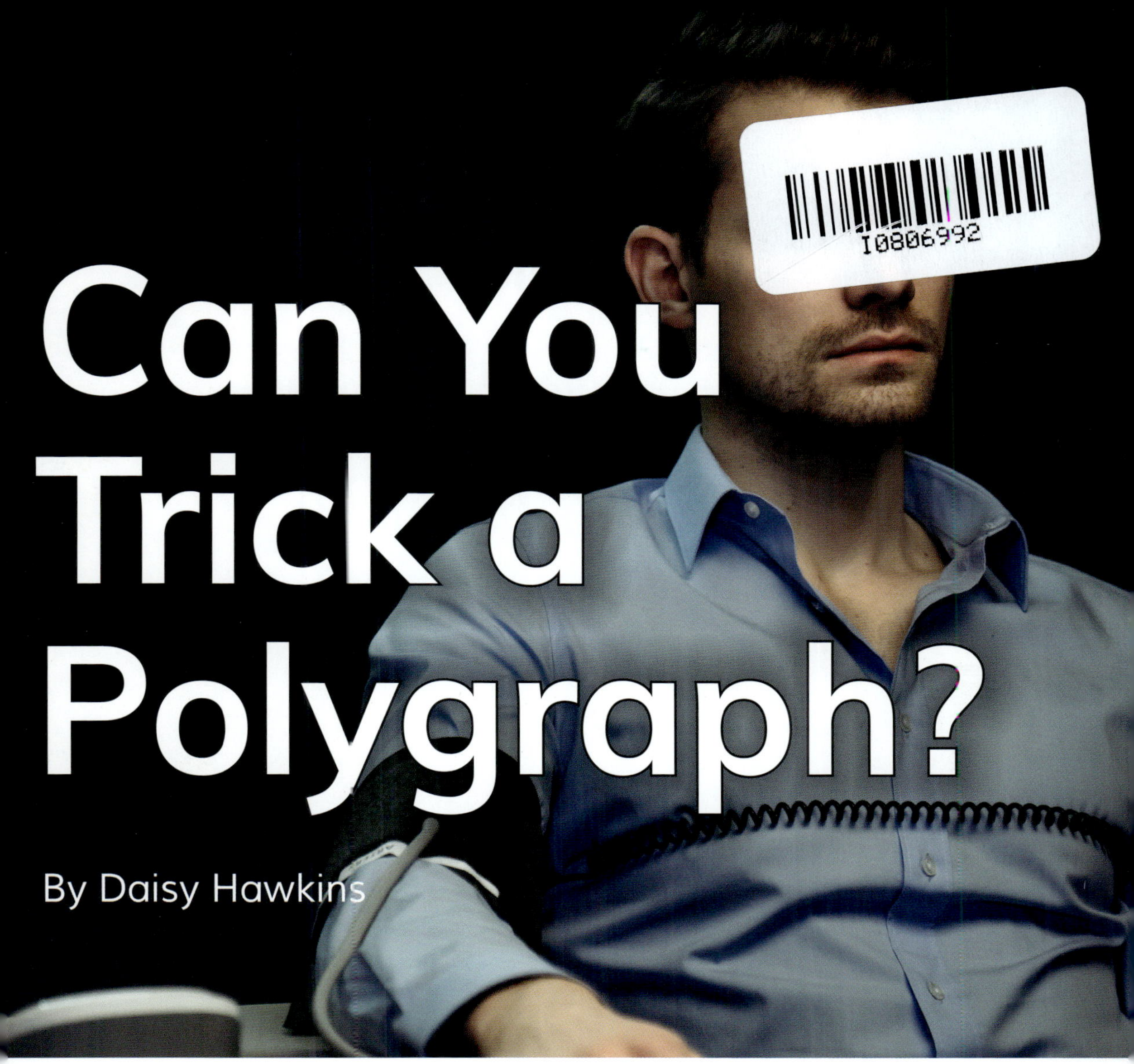

Can You Trick a Polygraph?

By Daisy Hawkins

Published in 2026 by
Norwood House Press
2544 Clinton Street
Buffalo, NY 14224

Printed in the United States of America

Library of Congress Cataloging-in-Publication Data:
Names: Hawkins, Daisy, author. | Rooney, Anne, author. | Brown, Alan, illustrator.
Title: Can you trick a polygraph? / by Daisy Hawkins. Space invaders / written by Anne Rooney, illustrated by Alan Brown.
Description: Buffalo, NY : Norwood House Press, 2026. | Series: Phonics all-stars: phase 5c
Identifiers: ISBN 9781978578173 (pbk.) | ISBN 9781978578180 (library bound) | ISBN 9781978578197 (ebook)
Subjects: LCSH: Reading–Phonetic method–Juvenile literature. | English language–Phonetics–Juvenile literature. | Truthfulness and falsehood–Juvenile literature. | Video games–Juvenile fiction.
Classification: LCC LB1573.3 H395 2026 | DDC 372.465–dc23

CPSIA compliance information: Batch #CW26NHP: For further information contact Norwood House Press at 1-800-237-9932.

Can we trust everything people say?

Sadly, no. Sometimes people tell lies. (We are all human!)

Some lies are little.

Some lies are big.

It would be so useful if we could detect the big lies ...

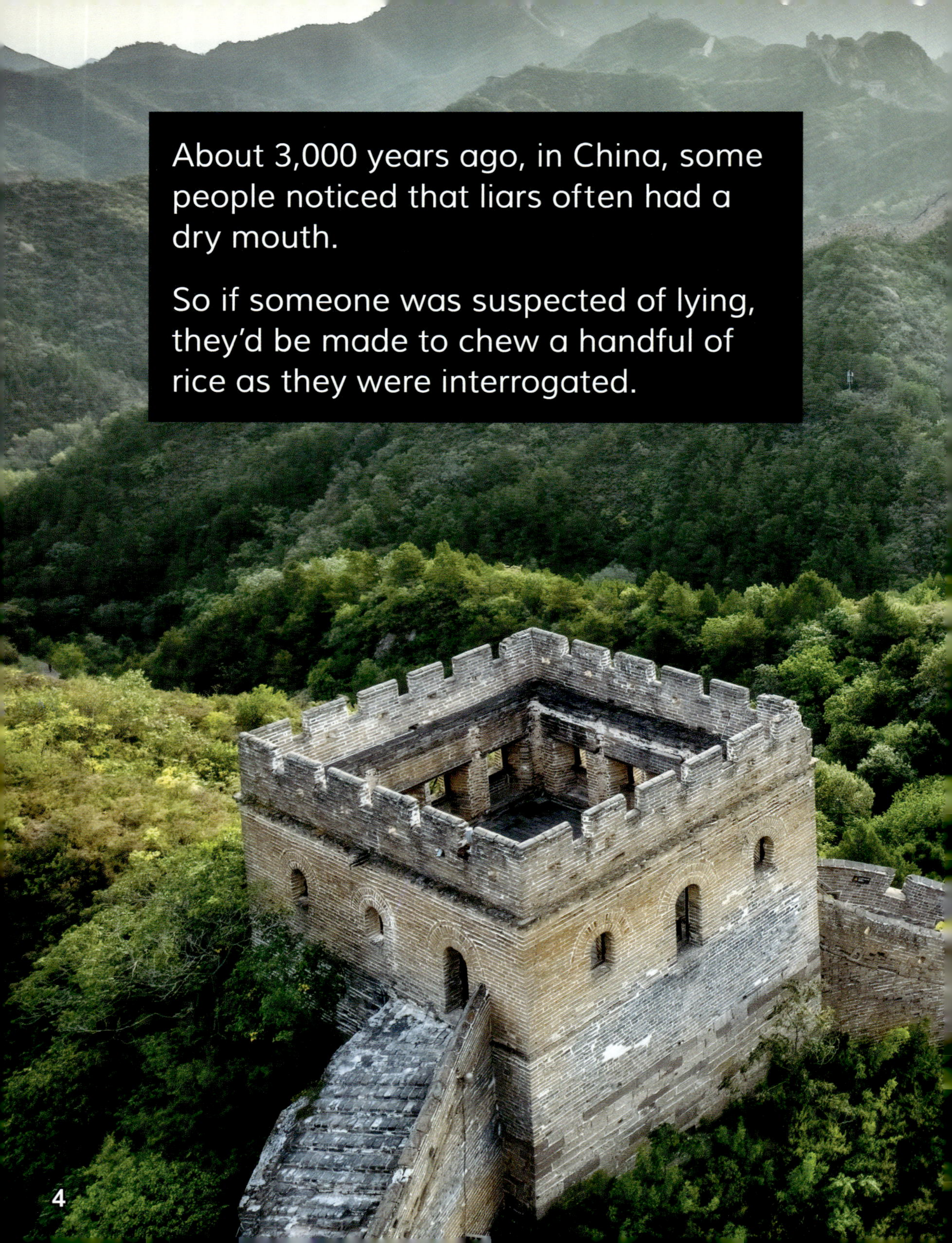

About 3,000 years ago, in China, some people noticed that liars often had a dry mouth.

So if someone was suspected of lying, they'd be made to chew a handful of rice as they were interrogated.

Then, later, they would spit the rice out.

If the rice was moist, the person was not lying.

If it was dry ...

Nowadays, we have something called a polygraph, or "lie-detector" test.

It is based on the same idea that the Chinese had. If you are lying, you will be stressed – and the polygraph can "see" this.

The polygraph picks up on cues from your body, such as:

- your breathing
- your pulse rate
- how much you sweat

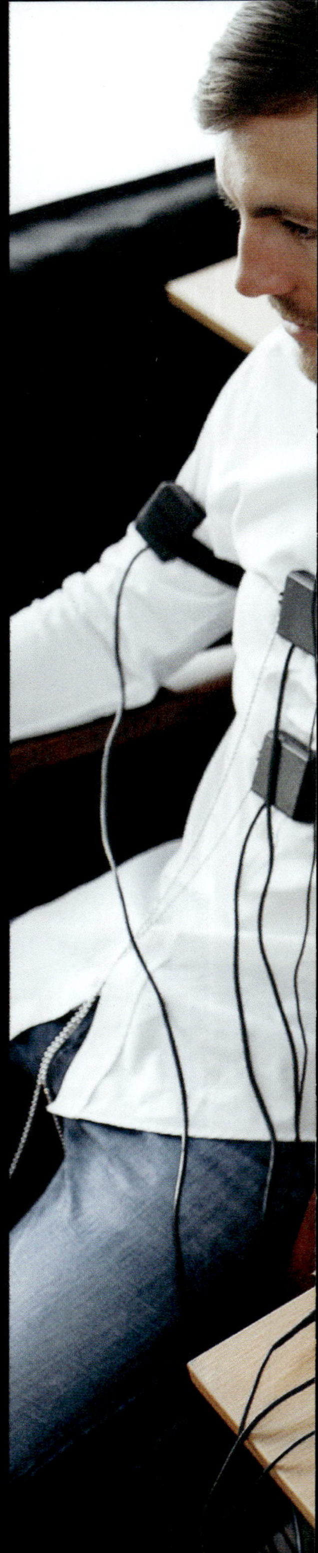

In a lie-detector test, a person starts by asking you things that you cannot lie about.

They record how your body responds.

Next, they ask you things that you might lie about. If your body responds just as before, the person can see that you are not lying now.

If your breathing gets faster, or if you start to sweat, then you are lying.

Polygraphs were used a lot by governments around the world. Some governments still use them.

Do they work? No, not really.

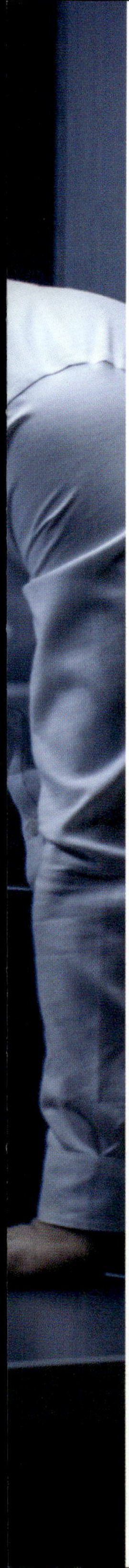

Some people get stressed if you ask them **anything**. So, for them, a lie will not show as anything different.

Some people **never** get stressed by anything – ever! So, for them too, a lie will not show as anything different.

Could someone trick a polygraph?

Probably, yes. You could sneak in some lies at the beginning of the test. So they think you are telling them facts, but you are not.

Yes.
Well, in fact it's Joseph. So I'm lying right now!

Many spies have been able to trick a lie-detector test.

For example, this man was an American spy who handed secrets over to another power. Yet he passed a number of polygraph tests.

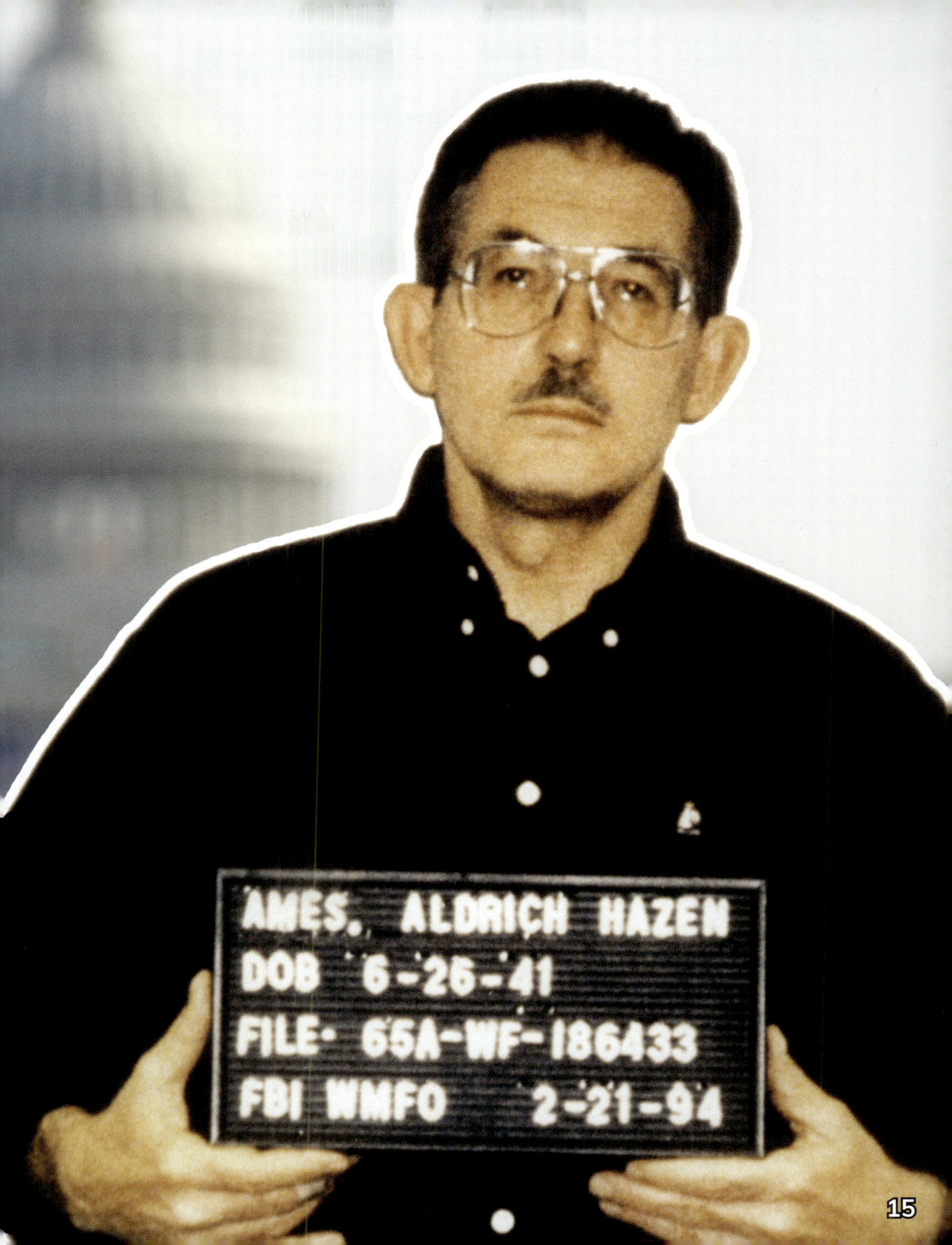
AMES, ALDRICH HAZEN
DOB 6-26-41
FILE- 65A-WF-186433
FBI WMFO 2-21-94

So is it possible to **trick** a lie-detector test? Yes, it's certainly possible!

Can we **trust** a lie-detector test? No, not really.

In which case, there is really no need to try to trick it in the first place!

Space Invaders

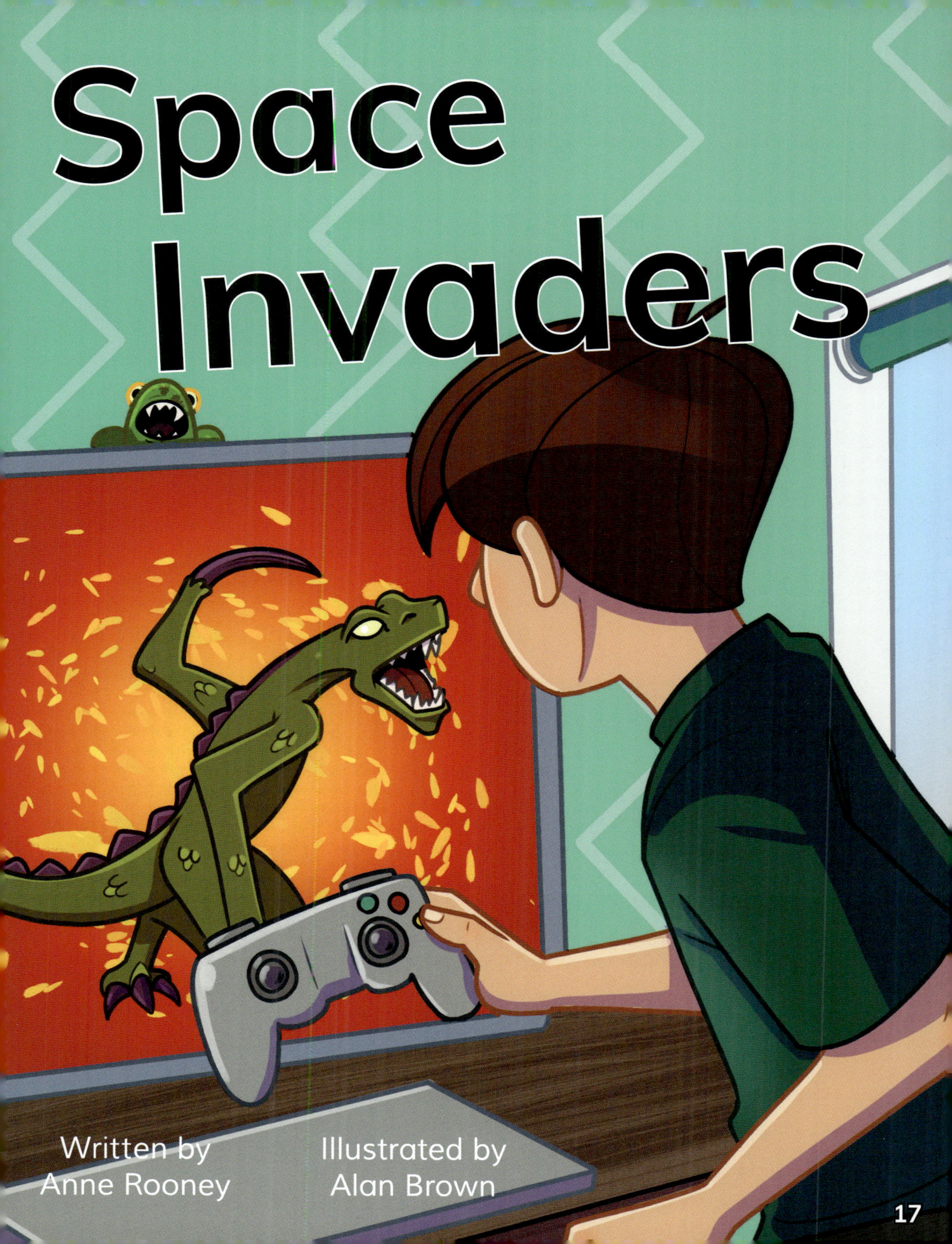

Written by
Anne Rooney

Illustrated by
Alan Brown

Todd threw off his coat and turned on the computer. He had a new game.

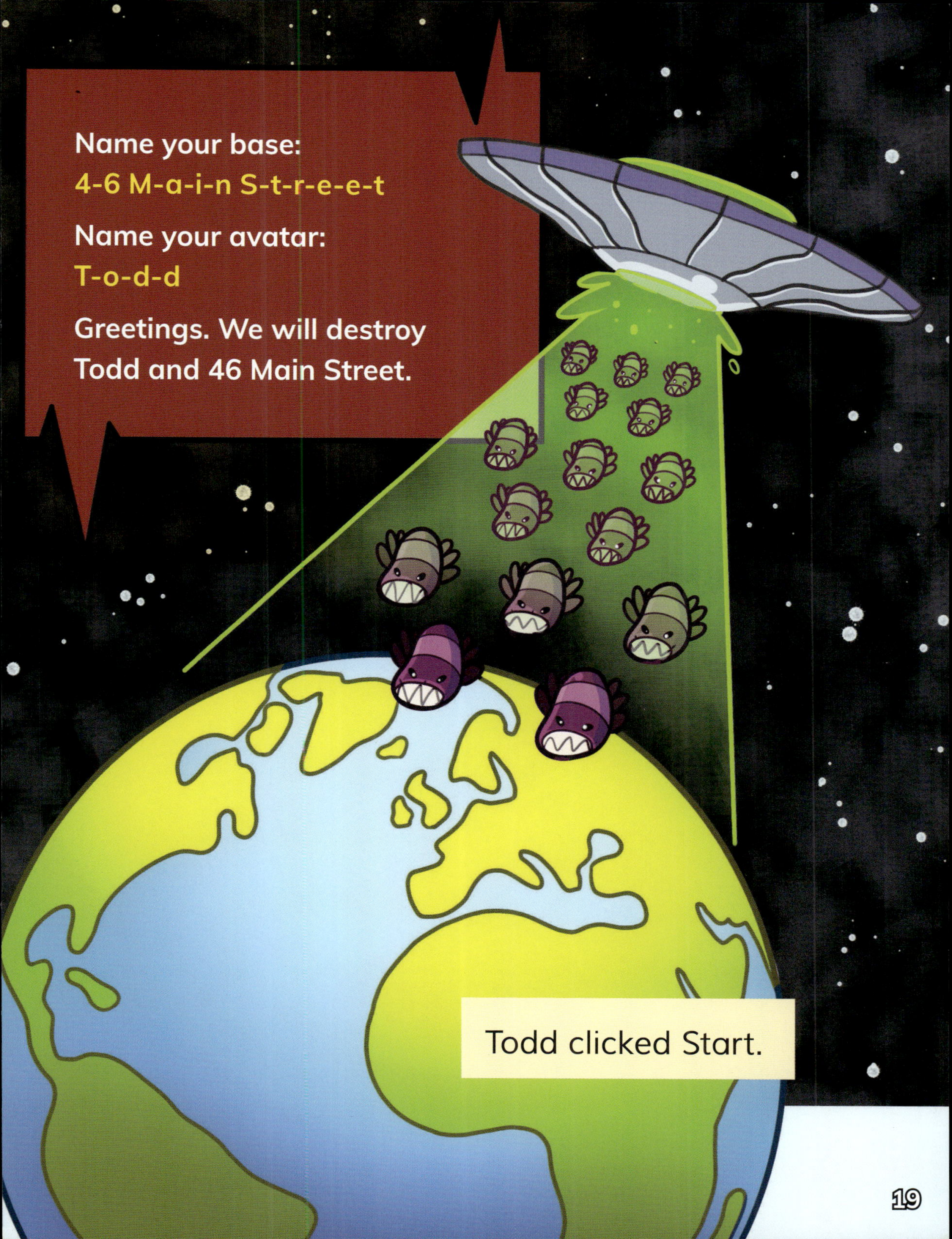

Todd clicked Start.

The screen zoomed in on Todd's base. A line of tiny purple bugs approached it.

He spent three credits on bug spray. Foam covered the bugs, but they did not die.

Todd slapped at a tickle on his arm. The squished bug was an odd shade of pink. He wiped it with his hand.
Second attack!
Todd! Food!

Todd heard something scuttle across the room.

He groaned. Would he have to coax his mouse back into its cage again?

Todd gobbled a poached egg on toast, then raced back to his room.

Small green shapes like toads with tails roamed his computer screen.

Todd purchased roach gas for five credits.

The gas made the toad-like monsters grow wider and taller.

They grew wings and floated up into the air, sailing over his space base.

Todd jumped as something flew into the window with a thud.

Stupid birds, he thought.

He turned the screen off and went to bed.

In the morning, Todd turned on the screen.

There were monsters everywhere.

Todd spent his last credits and blasted the monsters, but they kept coming.

Something bellowed on the road outside.

On the screen, a monster leered at him, raising an arm with hooked claws. Todd moaned.
Fourth attack!
Space cannon – 40 credits.

Todd didn't have forty credits. What could he do?
Credit loan?
End game?

That was it!

Todd clicked on End game.

Todd clicked **No**.

Mom looked into his room. She groaned.

"What happened here?"

"Um ... a bird hit the window," Todd said.

The carpet was soaked with bug foam.

Todd thought he would delete **Space Invaders**. Perhaps he would play **ZombieZone** now.